OPRAH WINFREY

A Voice for the People
by Philip Brooks

A Book Report Biography
FRANKLIN WATTS
A Division of Grolier Publishing
New York / London / Hong Kong / Sydney
Danbury, Connecticut

For my dear friend Kelly Knight, who overcame difficult beginnings to become another woman of great humor, humanity, and strength

frontispiece: Oprah Winfrey at a showing of her TV special
Before Women Had Wings

Cover illustration by Janet Hamlin,
interpreted from a photograph © Gamma Liaison/Steve Allen

Photographs ©: AP/Wide World Photos: 10 (Steve Green), 103 (Novovitch), 19, 27, 55, 67, 99, 100; Corbis-Bettmann: 89 (Reuters), 47 (UPI), 36, 42, 43; David M. Carter: 82; Gamma-Liaison: 96 (Barry King), 111; Globe Photos: 114 (Tim Anderson), 105 (Judie Burstein), 16 (George Koshollek Jr.), 76 (Lynn McAfee), 2 (Lisa Rose), 74 (Adam Scull), 45 (Robert Trendler), 64; Magnum Photos: 40 (Wayne Miller); Photofest: 92 (Gregory Heisler), 78 (Gordon Parks), 85; Sygma: 109 (Henry Bargas), 31, 79.

Visit Franklin Watts on the Internet at:
http://publishing.grolier.com

Library of Congress Cataloging-in-Publication Data

Brooks, Philip, 1963–
    Oprah Winfrey : a voice for the people / by Philip Brooks
        p. cm.—(A book report biography)
    Includes bibliographical references and index.
    Summary: Follows the life of the successful entertainer Oprah Winfrey, from her difficult childhood to her present fame.
    ISBN 0-531-11563-1 (lib. bdg.)   0-531-16406-3 (pbk)
    1. Winfrey, Oprah—Juvenile literature. 2. Television personalities—United States—Biography—Juvenile literature. 3. Motion picture actors and actresses—United States—Biography—Juvenile literature. [1. Winfrey, Oprah. 2. Television personalities. 3. Actors and actresses. 4. Afro-Americans—Biography. 5. Women—Biography.]
I. Title II. Series
PN1992.4.W56B76 1999
791.45'028'092—dc21
    [B]   98-35382
                                          CIP
                                          AC

 © 1999 by Franklin Watts, a division of Grolier Publishing
All rights reserved. Published simultaneously in Canada
Printed in the United States of America
1 2 3 4 5 6 7 8 9 10 R 08 07 06 05 04 03 02 01 00 99

GROLIER
PUBLISHING

CONTENTS

OPRAH WINFREY

CHAPTER ONE

A WOMAN OF INFLUENCE

In 1989, Oprah Winfrey was honored as *Ms.* magazine's Woman of the Year. Author Maya Angelou, one of Winfrey's mentors, wrote a tribute in which she said: "Oprah, as a talk-show host, tries to manage a calm facade as she lends an ear to brutes, bigots, and bagmen, but her face betrays her. Her eyes fill with tears when she listens to the lament of mothers mistreated by their offspring, and they dart indignantly at the report of cruelty against children and savagery against the handicapped. The even, full lips spread into a wide-open smile when a guest or audience member reveals a daring spirit and a benevolent wit."

For millions of Americans, Oprah Winfrey is much more than the host of a television show. As the richest and arguably most influential African-American woman in U.S. history, she is seen by many as proof that if you work hard enough, and

As the host of The Oprah Winfrey Show,
*Winfrey has become one of the most influential
people in the United States.*

are true to your own spirit, you will be accepted and will excel no matter the color of your skin, the size of your body, or your background. Winfrey puts it this way: "If you seek what is honorable, what is good, what is the truth of your life, all the other things you could not imagine come as a matter of course." Oprah has struggled most of her life to find the truth of her self and has allowed her viewers to share that search.

"If you seek what is honorable . . . all the other things you could not imagine come as a matter of course."

Born to a poor single mother in rural Mississippi, Winfrey has risen to become one of the most respected and admired people in the United States. In truth, her opinions are often more influential than those of the president. Every day, millions tune in to hear her thoughts on topics ranging from beauty makeovers to human rights.

CHAPTER TWO

OPRAH'S BEGINNINGS

Born on January 29, 1954, Oprah Winfrey was actually supposed to have been named "Orpah" after a character in the Bible's book of Ruth. But when the town's midwife, a woman who helps other women during childbirth, accidentally transposed two letters on her birth certificate, she became Oprah instead.

Though she often makes sure to mention the good times as well as the bad, Oprah Winfrey had a terribly difficult childhood. She suffered regular abuse, both physical and emotional, as well as grinding poverty. Still, Oprah grew into a strong young woman with a deep belief in her own worth. This was thanks in large part to the love and invaluable support of a few adults: her deeply religious grandmother, her strong-willed father, and a few special teachers.

Most of Oprah's earliest memories are of her grandmother's pig farm in Kosciusko, Mississippi. When her mother, Vernita, moved north to Milwaukee, Wisconsin, she left Oprah behind. She was cared for by her grandmother Hattie Mae. Oprah loved her grandmother and feared her grandfather, Henry "Earless" Lee. "I remember him always throwing things at me or trying to shoo me away with his cane." The three lived in an old three-room house without plumbing, isolated from their neighbors and the world outside of Mississippi. "I never had a store-bought dress," she remembers. "We grew everything we ate. We sold eggs. It was very lonely out there in the country." Since she lived on a muddy farm, Winfrey never wore shoes except when she went to church on Sundays.

Despite little interaction with other children, Oprah was a sociable child. She was also very smart. By the time she was three years old, she knew how to read and loved to talk about stories in the Bible or about the animals she helped care for. But her grandparents believed children should be "seen and not heard." So when company came, Oprah generally had to sit quietly in a corner and listen to the adults. When she was allowed to speak, Oprah shined. Visitors were impressed with little Oprah and this made Hattie Mae proud. Though Hattie Mae was stern and strict, she always let Oprah know that she loved her.

When she was three years old, Oprah began reciting passages from the Bible at the Faith United Mississippi Baptist Church. The old whitewashed church, sun pouring in through the windows and wasps droning above the slow-turning ceiling fans, holds a powerful spot in Winfrey's memory. "The sisters sitting in the front row would fan themselves and nod to my grandmother Hattie Mae. And they'd say, 'Hattie Mae, this child is gifted.' And somehow, with no education, my grandmother instilled in me a belief that I could aspire to do great things in my life." In fact, Oprah credits Hattie Mae with making her who she is. She happily remembers sleeping with her grandmother in an old featherbed and swinging together on the porch swing outside the front door. To this day, when she thinks of her childhood, those times on the porch are when she felt most happy, safe, and loved. "I am what I am because of my grandmother. My strength. My sense of reasoning. Everything. All of that was set by the time I was six years old. I basically am no different now from what I was when I was six."

Hattie Mae mixed the sweet comforts of the porch swing and featherbed with large doses of harsh and cruel punishment. Time after time, Oprah was sent out to find a "switch," a flexible tree branch stripped of its leaves, that would be used to give her a whipping. "In the middle of the whipping," Oprah remembers, "you hear 'Now shut up, shut up!' You couldn't even cry! You got whipped till you had welts on your back. Unbelievable. I used to get them every day because I was very precocious. I was always getting into trouble and I always thought I could get away with it . . . . She could whip me for days and never get tired. It would be called child abuse now." In those days, such whippings were a regular part of the way many African-Americans raised their children, Winfrey has pointed out. African-American comedian Richard Pryor has talked often about being sent out to get the switch with which he would be disciplined. He called it "the loneliest walk in the world." Winfrey remembers looking at little white girls in town and wishing she could be white too so that she could escape the switch. She would even go so far as to put a clothespin on her nose at night in an attempt to make her nose look more Caucasian.

LIFE IN MILWAUKEE

When Oprah was seven years old, she was forced to leave the world she knew and the grandmother she loved. Vernita Lee demanded that Oprah be sent to live with her in Milwaukee. Working as a

Milwaukee, Wisconsin, was Oprah Winfrey's home, on and off, during her early years.

cleaning woman, Vernita earned just $50 a week and already had another child living in her tiny apartment. Oprah felt like a further burden on her struggling mother and wondered why she had been taken away from the open spaces and clean air of the farm to live in a dingy apartment in a cold, dark, northern city.

Milwaukee offered all sorts of things to do, like seeing movies and eating pizza, but Oprah never had any money. Stuck in the apartment all the time, she even resorted to catching cockroaches in a jar for fun, making pets out of them, and watching their furious attempts to escape. Angry at her mother for bringing her to Milwaukee and just plain bored, Oprah stole money from her mother's purse. "I wanted to have money like all the other kids," she recalled. Stealing soon became a bad habit.

In contrast to her difficulties at home, Oprah excelled in school. One day in kindergarten she wrote her teacher a note that said: "Dear Miss New: I do not think I belong here." The teacher quickly saw to it that Oprah was moved into first grade. A year later Oprah decided to skip another grade. "I didn't think it was necessary to go to second grade, so I told my teacher and was moved into third grade. I couldn't stand to be bored."

Oprah had grown into a strong-willed little girl who always liked to be in charge and enjoyed being the center of attention. She continued to give Bible readings in church and became a leader in school. "If I was playing school, I wouldn't play unless I was the teacher. Or we didn't play house unless I was the mama . . . I came from a matriarchal family so I had to be the mama and had to tell the daddy what to do." Also, Oprah had begun to display what can only be described as "charisma," an unexplainable ability to command the attention of large numbers of people.

More and more, Oprah began to understand her abilities as a public speaker and began to use these strengths to make people do what she believed was right. Even at a young age, she understood how language and tone of voice could be used to make other people feel and understand things that were important to her. One day a group of bigoted white children threatened to beat her up: "So I told them about Jesus of Nazareth and what happened to the people who tried to stone him. The kids called me the Preacher and left me alone after that." Oprah had not used the story of Jesus simply to get herself out of trouble. She had made her schoolmates feel the truth of a story that had moved her. Oprah's faith touched them in some way that made them decide not to hurt her, and to respect her as a human being forever after, rather than seeing her as "a black girl."

FROM MILWAUKEE TO NASHVILLE

In 1962, when Oprah was eight years old, her mother decided she could no longer support or control her energetic, intelligent, and mischievous daughter. Desperate for help, she arranged for Oprah to take a bus to Tennessee. It was a journey that would turn Oprah's life in a better direction. Vernon Winfrey awaited Oprah's arrival at the station in Nashville.

Vernon was Oprah's father. He and Vernita had been boyfriend and girlfriend during high school. Vernita had become pregnant with his child while they were still teenagers, but they never married. Before Vernita gave birth to Oprah, Vernon had joined the army and moved away from Mississippi. When Vernon was discharged from the service in 1955, he settled in Nashville. Opportunities were few for black men

Oprah enjoyed living with her father and stepmother in Nashville, Tennessee.

living in the American South. Racism was an accepted fact of life. There were certain jobs for which blacks were seen as qualified and others for which they were not. Vernon worked for a while as a dishwasher earning 75 cents an hour. Eventually he was hired as a maintenance man at Vanderbilt University. Such work was steady and respectable. And Vernon, who along with his wife, Zelma, valued education, was proud to be connected to a fine university—even if it was one he would not have been permitted to attend. Vernon later became a barber and shopkeeper.

For the first time in her life, Oprah lived in a stable and loving home where her mind was stimulated and she was free from whippings, poverty, and loneliness. Vernon and Zelma were quiet people, not prone to displays of affection, but Oprah felt cared for, valued, and respected. Vernon and Zelma saw immediately that eight-year-old Oprah had the potential to be an exceptional person, and they held her to the highest standards. In Nashville, the self-discipline that grandmother Hattie Mae had instilled allowed Oprah to meet the intellectual and spiritual challenges Vernon and Zelma set for her.

Oprah was excited by Vernon and Zelma's expectations, and she flourished as never before. When Zelma discovered that Oprah was bad at math, she spent the entire summer drilling her on her multiplication tables. "My stepmother was real tough, a real strong disciplinarian, and I owe a lot to her because it was like military school there. I had to do book reports at home as well as in school and so many vocabulary words a week. That's what we did." While Oprah wished she could spend more time playing outside, she basked in the attention Zelma lavished on her and rewarded her stepmother's patience with consistent achievement.

"My stepmother was real tough. . . . I had to do book reports at home as well as in school and so many vocabulary words."

Vernon and Zelma also reinforced Oprah's strong connection to the Baptist Church. For many blacks, in the South especially, the church was a focal point for community activities. One of the things that gave Oprah the most joy in her "new life" with her father and stepmother was the career goal they set for her. It was decided she would be a missionary. Today, she can laugh at how zealous she became: "I wanted to be a missionary for the longest time! I was a missionary for Costa Rica, let me tell you. I used to collect money on the playground every single day of the year. I was a maniac."

She also continued to give regular recitations at church. She often performed William Ernest Henley's poem "Invictus":

Out of the night that covers me,
Black as the Pit from pole to pole,
I thank whatever gods may be,
For my unconquerable soul.

Sadly, the comfort and security she had found in Nashville lasted only a year.

BACK TO MILWAUKEE

In 1963, Vernita wrote a letter to Vernon Winfrey telling him she wanted her daughter back. She was about to be remarried and planned to reunite her children and make a fresh start. Oprah was understandably upset about returning to Milwaukee, but she also hoped that maybe this time things would be better with her mother. "The reason was that my mother would say, 'Come live with me. I'm gonna get married and we're gonna be a real family.' This guy she'd been dating for years, he's also the father of my brother. So that's why I stayed; I wanted a normal family. It never worked out, though."

When Oprah visited friends who had mothers and fathers living in the same house, she felt all the worse. "I used to make up stories about my mother and my dad," she remembers. "I told the biggest lies about them because I wanted to be like everybody else." Today, many children live with only one of their parents. But that was not the case in those days.

Adding to her bad feelings about having a disjointed family was the dawning realization that the color of her skin mattered. In Milwaukee, even within the black community, she began to feel subtle discrimination: "I felt really ugly in this environment because I believed the lighter your complexion, the prettier you were. My new sister was lighter and she got all the attention and I thought it was because she was the prettiest."

•Oprah was also made to feel uncomfortable about her high achievement in school. "I was the smartest, but no one praised me for being smart. I was teased because I was always sitting in the corner reading—people made fun of me for that. And I felt really sad and left out. My books were my only friends." Oprah was enduring what many intelligent girls feel. Many images of women on television, in the movies, and in magazines teach girls to be pretty and quiet, not smart and boisterous. Too often these "hidden messages" and peer pressure force talented young women like Oprah to question their ambitious dreams and to lose confidence in themselves. Such a loss of self-esteem is devastating. Oprah fought her whole life to be her true self rather than what other people wanted her to be.

OPRAH AND HER MOM

Growing up, Oprah was very angry with her mother. Vernita, working as a maid, had to struggle just to put food on the table and had little time to love and nurture her children. Even today Oprah feels some anger toward her mother because of this lack of affection. "I was the kind of kid who would have benefited from hugging. But she doesn't understand that, and I can't change that." But not all of her memories of her mother are bad. She credits her mother with making her understand the importance of one's appearance. Along with Oprah's intelligence and speaking ability, she has always had a sense of how one ought to dress and carry oneself in order to be seen as a strong and valuable person. "My mother was the best-dressed maid ever known to woman. You know how you see women going to work at the nice white people's houses wearing slacks? My mother would put on high-heel shoes and her suede skirt and go steppin'. It was very important for her not to look the part. She'd get her hair done and go to work."

A DARK SECRET

Oprah dealt with some difficult times in Milwaukee, but things were about to get much worse. When she was nine years old, Oprah was often left in the care of a nineteen-year-old male cousin. He would take care of Oprah when her mother was busy. Oprah never felt comfortable with him, especially when she stayed the night and they had to share a bed. One night, the young man forced Oprah to have sex with him. "I knew it was bad and I knew it was wrong," Oprah remembered. "Mainly because it hurt so badly. He took me to get ice cream and to the zoo afterward, and he told me if I ever told, we would both get in trouble. So I never did. It was in the summer of my ninth year. . . . So that's why I weep for the lost innocence. I weep for that because you are never the same again."

To this day, Oprah has not revealed the name of the cousin who raped her. Tragically, this was not to be the last sexual abuse she suffered. "It happened over a period of years, between nine and fourteen. It happened at my own house, by different people—this man, that man . . . I remember blaming myself for it, thinking something must be wrong with me." She was especially crushed when a favorite uncle molested her. "I adored this uncle. Just adored him. And I could not, in my mind, make him be the bad guy." Oprah never felt she could tell anyone about these abuses. She believed that the rest of her family would think she was lying or was somehow responsible. Later, when she learned on the school playground that sex was what made women have babies, she worried constantly that she was pregnant. How, she wondered, would she hide her shameful secret from her classmates and her family? And how would she care for a baby? These are not the sort of heavy emotional burdens a nine-year-old girl should have to carry.

Perhaps the most troubling aspect of these crimes was that Oprah—at such a young age—began to blame herself, rather than the twisted men who had violated her. Emotional scars created by their actions led to terrible problems in Oprah's life for decades to come. It is a tribute to Winfrey's strength and generous heart that she has not seen fit to reveal their names in the press.

Winfrey hid the fact that she had been a victim of abuse for many years. Then, in 1985, a guest on her show was speaking with great emotion about having been sexually abused by relatives as a child. Winfrey, suddenly unable to contain herself, revealed her secret at last. "We were doing a show on the subject, and ... the phones lit up with calls from women all over the

*Winfrey's success as a talk-show host is due in part to
her willingness to reveal herself, both her strengths
and weaknesses, on national television.*

country saying the same thing had happened to them as girls. The guest I was interviewing started crying, and I started crying and told for the first time that it had happened to me too." Women across the country were moved and thankful. Oprah said later, "I no longer had to live with this horrible secret, and I knew it could help others who had suffered the same way."

As the years went by, Winfrey learned that the abuse she suffered as a girl had led to emotional trouble throughout her life including a number of self-destructive relationships with men. Even gaining a lot of weight could be traced to a desire to create a kind of protective coating inside which she could hide. Millions of U.S. women watched as Winfrey slowly discovered how profoundly these terrible violations of trust had affected her and continued to haunt her life. Winfrey's long healing process, as it unfolded on national TV, brought the subject into the public eye and revealed how widespread the problem of childhood sexual abuse remains. Because of Winfrey's courage and honesty, thousands of women broke their silence about abuses they had suffered or knew about. Also, new awareness of the problem has helped teachers, police, and caregivers to recognize signs of abuse so that they can help children in trouble.

A STAR STUDENT

When Vernon Winfrey sent Oprah to Milwaukee for the summer, he had promised he would bring her back to Nashville in time for the beginning of the next school year. But in September, Vernita refused to send her daughter back to him. Vernon threatened to call the police, but Vernita reminded him that he had never officially been named Oprah's father. Because he had never legally been named a parent or guardian, he had no power to force Vernita to relinquish her hold on Oprah despite continuing problems in the household.

Though he knew nothing of Oprah's sexual abuse, Vernon knew Vernita was not a fit parent at that difficult point in her life. He remembers the frustration of feeling utterly powerless to help his daughter: "We had brought her out of that atmosphere, out of a house and into a home. No, I knew it was not good for her being in that environment again."

Despite her sorrow and anger at not returning to Nashville, Oprah continued to do well in school. She loved to be in school. Teachers provided the positive support she did not get at home. "I felt it happen in the fourth grade. Something came over me. I turned in a book report early and it got such a good response, I thought, 'I'm gonna do that again.'"

In fact, Oprah considers fourth grade to have been one of the turning points in her life. She never forgot her fourth-grade teacher, Mrs. Duncan. "There was always one teacher who stuck out as your favorite, be it the teacher who made you work the hardest, the one who gave you all the breaks, or maybe the one who just brought out the best in you." Mrs. Duncan made Oprah want to become a fourth-grade teacher when she grew up. She helped restore Oprah's confidence in herself.

"There was always one teacher who stuck out as your favorite, be it the teacher who made you work the hardest, the one who gave you all the breaks, or maybe the one who just brought out the best in you."

When Oprah was thirteen, another important teacher would change her life. Eugene Abrams used to notice her reading in the school cafeteria and took a special interest in her. He worked hard to get her a scholarship to Nicolet, a fine private school about 25 miles (40 km) outside Milwaukee. At Nicolet, nearly all the students were white and came from upper-middle-class homes. But the atmosphere did not intimidate Winfrey. In fact, she became a leader in

During her childhood, some of Oprah's well-meaning friends would ask if she knew Sammy Davis, Jr., and other African-Americans, just because they shared a skin color.

school. She did well in her studies and was extremely popular.

FEELING DIFFERENT

But when a number of her new classmates began inviting her to their homes for dinner, Oprah felt the gap that existed between their lives and hers. Though these friends meant well, they often made her uncomfortable. Well-meaning but clumsy efforts to make her feel "at home" frequently backfired and were unintentionally insulting. Her hosts played music by black artists or talked about popular black performers such as Sammy Davis, Jr., as if she knew them personally. Others introduced her to black butlers and maids who worked in their homes, believing Oprah might know them simply because they shared the same skin color.

Beyond issues of race and class, visits to these tidy homes filled with "normal" families made Oprah all the more unhappy about her own situation. She began to see herself as an "ugly poor girl." She wanted to be able to go to the pizza parlor and go to movies and play tennis like her friends. She began stealing money from her mother's purse again and staying out too late at night. She also began to be sexually active with the boys she met on such adventures. All of the abuse she had suffered—her sadness, loneliness, and need for affection—made her vulnerable to boys who seemed to care about her.

CHAPTER THREE

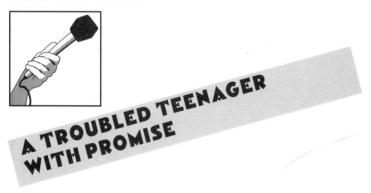

A TROUBLED TEENAGER WITH PROMISE

When Oprah Winfrey found out she needed eyeglasses, she wanted the same fancy frames her friends at Nicolet wore. Her mother could not afford such a luxury and insisted that Oprah wear plain and less expensive eyeglasses. On the bus ride home from the optician, Oprah grew more resentful and would not wear the glasses. Alone at home, Oprah became so enraged, so frustrated, that she smashed her new glasses and then began destroying the furniture in the apartment. When she calmed down, she was horrified at what she had done. Her mother would be home from work soon, so Oprah decided to tell a lie. Instead of admitting what she had done, Oprah called the police, claiming she had been the victim of a burglary. Pressed for details, Oprah said she had taken a blow to the head from an intruder and now had amnesia. Though the police were doubtful, Oprah avoided punishment.

A few months later, Vernita decided that a stray puppy Oprah had adopted was unmanageable and would have to be given away. Oprah staged another robbery, this time pitching all of Vernita's jewelry out the window and claiming the dog had heroically foiled the burglars' plans. Oprah had used that story one time too many. Though it is funny today, such lies were the beginning of a bad period for Oprah. Her life began to spin out of control.

A RUNAWAY

In 1968, when she was fourteen years old, Oprah decided to run away from home. She packed a shopping bag with her clothes and headed for a friend's house. When she found the friend was not home, she wandered the streets. As she walked along, she watched a long, gleaming limousine swing to the curb outside a fancy hotel. Oprah stared, trying to imagine owning something so beautiful.

Then the chauffeur jumped out of the car and opened the passenger door. When singer Aretha Franklin stepped out of the car, Oprah saw an opportunity. She immediately began sobbing alligator tears and attracted Franklin's attention. Oprah spun a tale of worthy of one of Franklin's own hard-luck songs. Abandoned and alone in Milwaukee, she desperately needed money for a

Aretha Franklin was generous to a young runaway named Oprah Winfrey.

bus ticket back to her home in Ohio. Deeply moved, Franklin handed Oprah $100 and wished her luck. Rather than head for Ohio, Oprah used the money to rent a hotel room for a week. When the money ran out, she telephoned her minister who brought her back to Vernita. Her problems soon grew more serious.

Still fourteen, Oprah became pregnant and gave birth to a premature baby that did not survive. This chapter in Oprah's early years remained a family secret until it was revealed to the tabloids in 1990 by a half-sister who was well paid for her story. Revelation of this past mistake forced Winfrey to face a painful memory. "That experience was the most emotional, confusing, and traumatic of my young life. . . . Everybody in the family just sort of shoved it under a rock. Because I had been involved in sexual promiscuity, they thought if anything happened it had to be my fault."

Fed up with Oprah's lies and rebellious behavior, Vernita made a fateful decision. Desperate to make Oprah "mend her wicked ways," she tried to send her to a juvenile detention center: "I remember going to the interview process where they treat you like you're already a known convict and thinking to myself, how in the world is this happening to me? I was fourteen and I knew that I was a smart person; I knew I wasn't a bad person, and I remember thinking, 'How did this happen? How did I get here?'"

> "I knew I wasn't a bad person, and I remember thinking, 'How did this happen? How did I get here?'"

Fortunately for Oprah, Milwaukee's juvenile offender system was overloaded. Vernita was told there was a two-week wait for a place in a detention center. "My mother was so fed up with me at the time that she said, 'I can't wait two weeks. You've got to get out of my house now.'" In truth, Vernita loved her daughter and knew she simply could not provide the structure and guidance she obviously needed.

RETURN TO NASHVILLE

Vernita's decision to send Oprah back to Nashville is one for which Oprah is deeply thankful. Picking up right where they had left off, Vernon and Zelma Winfrey brought self-respect back into Oprah's life: "I'm grateful to my mother for sending me away. If she hadn't, I would have taken an absolutely different path in life."

During Oprah's years in Milwaukee, Vernon had opened a new barber shop and grocery store near the Faith United Baptist Church where he had become a deacon. The church's flock tended to stick together. When Oprah worked in the store, she met church members on an almost daily basis. People looked out for one another in the close-knit community. 'Oprah hated working in the store, "every minute of it," she has said. But she recognizes that it was this sort of responsibility that returned her to what she had been before her troubles in Milwaukee: a promising young woman. "I have a great father who used to tell me, 'Listen, girl, if I tell you a mosquito can pull a wagon, don't ask me no questions. Just hitch him up!' That's the kind of dad I had," she once told a reporter. "A very, very stern disciplinarian. It's because of him, I believe, I am where I am today."

Zelma also became involved in Oprah's development again. Every two weeks they went to the library together and chose five books. Oprah was expected to write a book report on each one. It was during this period that Oprah's lifelong love and respect for literature began. Two books especially became touchstones: Margaret Walker's *Jubilee* and Maya Angelou's *I Know Why the Caged Bird Sings*. Both books helped put Winfrey's own hardships into perspective, allowed her to see that her own life story also had meaning and joy in addition to the unhappiness she had known. "Reading gave me hope. For me it was the open door."

Maya Angelou, one of Oprah's favorite authors

Today, Oprah counts Maya Angelou among her best friends and most important teachers. Angelou calls Winfrey her "spiritual daughter."

INTEGRATION

In 1967, Nashville began to desegregate its public schools. Up until that year, blacks and whites rarely shared a school building. But now, students from poor black and middle-class neighborhoods were sometimes bused to better-equipped and more modern schools in wealthier neighborhoods. Not everyone at East High School welcomed Oprah Winfrey and the other black students who arrived for the first day of classes. For perhaps the first time in her life, Oprah felt she was disliked by certain people simply because of the color of her skin. Until her first days at East High, racism was mainly something that happened in the news. The tension affected her schoolwork. Oprah brought home a report card full of C's.

Vernon and Zelma were very disappointed. They instituted a strict new schedule that included more study time and less television watching. "There are three kinds of people," Vernon liked to remind his daughter. "Those who make things happen, those who watch, and those who are never sure what's happening." Oprah Winfrey was expected to make things happen. And soon, she

*In high school, Oprah sometimes gave readings
on Harriet Tubman (far left, with some of the
slaves she helped to free).*

began to bring about changes in East High. The
drama club gave her a chance to sharpen her
speaking and acting talent. She gave readings on
slavery fighters Sojourner Truth and Harriet Tubman as well as excerpts from her favorite book,
Margaret Walker's *Jubilee*. Many of the white students were deeply impressed by the struggles
described in Oprah's readings and softened their
harsh attitudes toward black people.

At one point, Oprah joined her church group
on a trip to Hollywood. Marveling at the famous

Sojourner Truth is among those historical figures Oprah holds in high esteem.

names on the stars lining the sidewalk in front of Grumman's Chinese Theater, Oprah told everyone that such a star would one day belong to her. Friends and family agreed. Her father said in an interview, "We knew she had a gift and talent to act and speak when she was nine years old. . . . She always loved the limelight."

Oprah was elected president of the Student Government Association and began dating the boy named "most popular" in East High's yearbook. In 1970, she was invited to the White House Conference on Youth in Estes Park, Colorado. At the conference, 500 business leaders discussed the lives and concerns of the assembled teenagers. That same year, she took first place in the Tennessee Forensic League Tournament where she gave a reading from *Jubilee*. She also won the Elks Club Oratorical Contest and was awarded a partial scholarship to Tennessee State University. To add to a great year, Winfrey was named East High's representative in a group of Outstanding Teenagers of America. The honor was bestowed based on her "academic excellence and community service."

BEAUTY PAGEANTS

In 1971, when Oprah was seventeen years old, she stood 5 feet 7 inches (170 cm) tall and weighed

When Oprah saw the sidewalk outside Grumman's Chinese Theater in Hollywood, she vowed she would one day have a star there as well.

135 pounds (61 kg). She had grown into an attractive and poised young woman. She had a collection of excellent report cards, was popular with her classmates, and showed talent as a public speaker.

When she saw an ad in the newspaper for contestants in the Miss Fire Prevention pageant, Oprah signed up. She was the only African-American contestant. Despite all her attributes, she had no dreams of winning. "I entered it as a fluke. I entered because, at the time, we were *Negroes* . . . we hadn't gotten *black* yet. So I was the only Negro in the . . . contest. I certainly never expected to win, because why would I?"

"So I was the only Negro in the . . . contest. I certainly never expected to win, because why would I?"

At one point in the pageant, judges asked each contestant what she hoped to do with her life. Oprah listened as the girls ahead of her described their plans. Many hoped to marry and raise a family. Others planned to help in a family business or attend college. Several talked about becoming teachers. On her way to the Elks Club that afternoon, Oprah had decided to say that she hoped to become a fourth-grade teacher. But as she stood on stage staring out at the crowd, she suddenly thought about television journalist Barbara Walters. Oprah had watched her that morning on the *Today Show*. Walters was the first woman to be taken seriously as a TV journalist. "I believe in truth," Winfrey heard herself telling the judges. "And I want to perpetuate truth. So I want to be a journalist." Oprah won the contest, the first black woman ever to do so.

Encouraged by the overwhelmingly positive publicity she received as Nashville's first black Miss Fire Prevention, Oprah entered the Miss

Barbara Walters, here as host of the Today *show, inspired Winfrey to become a journalist.*

Black Nashville contest. She won again. Her prize was a scholarship to Tennessee State University. Later, Oprah would almost regret winning the scholarship. TSU was just 7 miles (11 km) from her home and she wanted to be on her own, making her own decisions and building her own life without her father and stepmother looking over her shoulder all the time.

Becoming Miss Black Nashville meant Oprah would compete in the statewide contest for Miss Black Tennessee. Oprah had no doubts about her talent and poise. But she believed she could not compete against the other six young women when it came to beauty. A prejudice favoring light-skinned contestants was widely accepted. Since local publicity had helped her to win the Miss Black Nashville, Oprah figured she had no chance at becoming Miss Black Tennessee. She was wrong. When the sparkling crown was placed on her head and a bouquet of roses was thrust into her arms, she was as shocked as her rivals. "There were all these light-skinned girls—vanillas—and here I was a fudge child—real dark-skinned. And Lord were they upset, and I was upset for them. Really I was."

Thinking back to that time, Oprah is struck by how strongly such prejudices influenced her image of herself. "I was raised to believe that the lighter your skin, the better you were. I wasn't light-skinned, so I decided to be the best and the smartest." She had also nearly starved herself to get ready for the judges' scrutiny. "You could see my bones," she remembers.

Miss Black Tennessee continued to go to bed hungry and soon headed for Hollywood, California, to compete for the national Miss Black America crown. It was August 1972 and Winfrey, now eighteen years old, was shocked to realize how far she had gone in the world of beauty pageants. She had entered Nashville's Miss Fire Prevention contest on a whim, and now here she was about to be on national television representing Tennessee. She looked at herself in the mirror wearing the sash that read "Miss Black Tennessee" and had to laugh.

In Hollywood, each young woman was assigned a chaperone to keep an eye on her during the week's festivities. Dr. Janet Burch, Winfrey's chaperone, remembers Oprah's desire to succeed: "I have never seen anybody who wanted to do well as much as Oprah did. She used to talk about things like how one day she was going to be very, very, very wealthy. The thought always precedes the happening. If you really think you're going to be very wealthy, and very popular and prominent, and if you sincerely believe it, it's going to happen . . . Oprah had a knack. She was bold enough to seek the information she wanted to know . . . Oprah had no qualms about asking anybody for anything." Even as a teenager, Winfrey's charm and ease with all sorts of people carried her a long way.

During the preliminaries, Winfrey impressed her fellow contestants. She wore her hair up in a sophisticated style and modeled only the most tasteful clothes. But it was her quick wit and poise that made everyone decide she was the favorite to win. Then a strange thing happened: Oprah seemed to decide she did not want to win. During the contest, she let her hair down and put aside the elegant dress she had originally chosen. She wore a silly-looking frilly gown instead. For the talent competition, she performed a monologue dressed as an old woman. She had sabotaged herself.

Not even chosen as a finalist, Winfrey was jubilant. After the show, she tearfully kissed the winner, congratulated the runners-up, and said good-bye to all her new friends with no regrets. She had moved on in her life, and pageants were left behind. Her puzzled father said later, "That's just the way she is. Oprah makes her own decisions." Ultimately, Winfrey felt pageants were not worthy of her time and talents. The fact that they judged a woman mainly on her physical appearance made Winfrey uncomfortable, and she no longer wanted to be a part of such an institution.

A START IN BROADCASTING

Another reason she lost interest in beauty pageants was her budding career in radio. Winfrey went to a local radio station to pick up a watch that was part of her Miss Fire Prevention prize. There she met John Heidelberg, a disc jockey at the station. Heidelberg was immediately impressed with Winfrey's smooth voice and excellent diction. "Why don't you try out for a job reading the news?" he suggested. Winfrey assumed he was joking, but she was flattered. Heidelberg insisted, and Winfrey auditioned on the spot for WVOL's station manager. Although impressed, he was skeptical about hiring a precocious seventeen-year-old high school student. Heidelberg finally convinced him to give Winfrey a chance.

Vernon Winfrey was less easily convinced. Oprah had schoolwork to do. He also worried men at the station would try to take advantage of his pretty daughter. Eventually, after Oprah pleaded with him, promising she would not date anyone from the station or let her grades slip, he relented.

Winfrey began reading the news after school every half hour until 8:30 P.M. During her training period, she worked for free. But as soon as she had proven herself, the station began paying her $100 a week. This was a welcome addition to the household budget. Vernon saw the part-time job as a good way to help pay for Winfrey's upcoming college expenses. Though he could not predict what Oprah would ultimately do with her life, he told Winfrey again and again that she would "never become something without a college education."

Winfrey missed a day at the microphone so she could attend her senior prom. Her new boyfriend, Anthony Otey, had chaired the prom committee and Oprah served alongside him. The blue, silver, and white decorations simulated "An Evening Above the Clouds," the prom's theme. Vernon even lifted Oprah's strict curfew for the occasion.

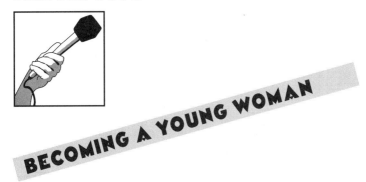

CHAPTER FOUR

BECOMING A YOUNG WOMAN

Oprah Winfrey began her college career at Tennessee State in 1972, a time of racial turmoil in the United States. Many black people had grown frustrated that the civil rights movement of Dr. Martin Luther King, Jr., Malcolm X, and others had not brought about more economic opportunities and social change. Some, especially disciples of Malcolm X and the nation of Islam, argued that the entire race should rise up in an armed revolution, overthrow the U.S. government, and take by force all that they deserved. Others wanted to create a separate country without white people to interfere with and thwart their hopes and dreams. Still others dreamed of a return to Africa, a mass exodus to "the motherland." Many more still honored the memory of Martin Luther King and remained convinced that blacks ought to continue raising their voices and working peacefully but vigorously within the present system to create change. Winfrey did not feel completely comfortable with any of these ideas.

While she firmly believed blacks had the right to equal opportunities, she had never felt denied such rights. "While they called me 'Oreo,' I remembered Jesse Jackson saying, 'Excellence is the best deterrent to racism.' So I pushed myself. In high school, I was the teacher's pet, which created other problems. I never spoke in African-American dialect—I'm not sure why, perhaps I was ashamed—and I was attacked for 'talking proper like white folks,' for selling out." Many African-Americans who speak standard English are made to feel this way.

In a climate of anger and youthful excitement, Winfrey seemed, to many of her classmates, uncommitted to the cause of civil rights. This was not true. But Winfrey was not the sort of person who wanted to be a political activist. Going to demonstrations and carrying signs was not her way of doing things. Further, she strongly disagreed with those who hated all white people. Despite the troubled times, she believed that whites and blacks had to see one another as individuals, as people, each one unique.

AT TENNESSEE STATE UNIVERSITY

The pressure to conform to other people's ideas made college an unhappy period for Winfrey. She

*Winfrey was encouraged by Jesse Jackson's comment
that "Excellence is the best deterrent to racism."*

later remembered: "It was 'in' to be angry. Whenever there was a conversation on race, I was on the other side; maybe I never felt the same kind of repression other black people are exposed to. I've not come up against obvious racism that I know of. I don't think, act, or live my life in racial terms." In fact, Oprah was wider read and better informed about black history than many of those who criticized her. But she believed these heroes of which she, as a black woman, was so proud, belonged to everyone, not only to black people. At a time when the United States seemed to be coming apart along racial lines, her beliefs were the exception. Having just left high school where she was voted "most popular girl," she found herself condemned by those around her. She was miserable and her grades began to suffer. "I hated, hated, hated college," she remembers.

Worse, she began the first in a series of failed romantic relationships that left her feeling helpless and unworthy of love. Today she understands that the sexual abuse she had suffered as a child caused her to choose the wrong kind of men, men incapable of giving her the affection and respect she needed and deserved.

Winfrey left college a few credits short of getting her degree. This pained Vernon Winfrey who worried about his daughter's future. In 1986, when she reenrolled at TSU, she worked with the faculty to prepare a project that would satisfy her media course requirement. When TSU informed her that she would receive her diploma during the 1987 commencement exercises, the administration also invited her to address the graduating class. In her speech, she told the graduates that her father had always said she would never amount to anything until she got a college degree. In cap and gown, she waved her diploma and blew a kiss to her father: "See, Daddy, I amounted to something," she said. That day she also endowed ten scholarships for students at TSU in her father's name. Vernon Winfrey could not have asked for a more glorious gift.

FIRST TIME ON TV

Winfrey continued to read the news on WVOL while she attended college. One day an executive from WTVF-TV, the local CBS affiliate, happened to hear the broadcast and asked her to audition for his television news show. Auditioning in front of cameras and lights was nerveracking. "I had no idea what to do or say. And I thought in my head that maybe I'll just pretend I'm Barbara Walters. I will hold my head like Barbara. So I crossed my legs at the ankles, and I put my little finger under my chin, and I leaned across the desk, and I pretended to be Barbara Walters."

The strategy worked well enough to land her a job as the first black person ever to be a news-show anchor on Nashville television. Still a sophomore at Tennessee State University, Winfrey hosted the weekend newscast and wrote her own scripts along with her co-anchor. Chris Clark, the news director, remembers that although he believed Winfrey to be a smart and talented person, she did not seem right for a job as a regular journalist: "She was real close to whatever she was doing and had a lot of sympathy and empathy for these people [whom] she was talking to . . . I'd send her out to do a cover story on a family that had just been burned out. She would give them money out of her pocket and cry half the day over this situation. She would take it personally." Winfrey agrees with his assessment: "I really agonized. I was a horrible writer, and I just broke down and cried with all those crime and fire stories. But I stuck it out because I figured one day it could lead to a talk show."

That is characteristic of Winfrey. Throughout her life, she has been able to recognize when a short-term opportunity might lead her closer to achieving a long-term goal. She understood, for instance, that beauty pageants could help her get an opportunity in show business.

Winfrey was also well aware that, beyond her talent, the station had hired her in order to put a black person's face on camera. "Sure I was a token," she says. "But, honey, I was a very happy token." She recognized that station executives were in some sense using her to make themselves look good, but she was also using them to get where she wanted to go. It was a good deal for all concerned.

> "Sure I was a token. But, honey, I was a very happy token."

✦ IN BALTIMORE

In 1976, Winfrey made another move designed to improve her long-term career. Baltimore was a much larger city than Nashville and therefore offered more exposure, so Winfrey took a job with a Baltimore station willing to make her its weekday evening co-anchor. Still only twenty-two years old, she remembers herself as "very naive." The new full-time, daily responsibility forced her to decide once and for all that she simply was not cut out to be a news anchor. Day after day, she found herself too emotionally involved with a story to act as a detached reporter. The station slowly came to the same conclusion. Station executives decided they had to get her out of the anchorperson's chair. But if they simply fired her, they would still have to pay the remainder of her contract. Besides, she was a nice enough kid and had a bit of talent. There had to be someplace on their schedule where they could use her.

On April 1, 1977, the station manager called Winfrey into his office and gave her the bad news. She was being taken off the newscast and made host of *People Are Talking*, WJZ-TV's morning talk show. Though the station manager did not tell her, the idea was to "hide" her on a show where she would not be noticed and see if she got any better on camera. Winfrey not only took her demotion in stride, she was relieved. "The first day I did [*People Are Talking*], I thought, 'This is what I really should have been doing all along.'"

THE MAKEOVER

The station had other ideas on how to improve Winfrey. What occurred as a result is very funny in retrospect but was an ordeal when it happened.

Some of the big shots at WJZ-TV felt she needed a "makeover." At a meeting, they informed Winfrey that her hair was too thick and too long. They did not stop with her hairdo: "They came to me and said, 'Your eyes are too far apart, your nose is too wide, your chin is too wide, and you need to do something about it.' So they sent me to New York, to a chichi, poo-poo, la-di-da salon—the kind that serves you wine so that when you leave it doesn't matter what you look like. . . . So this Frenchman put a French perm in my black hair. I was the kind of woman at that time—this was 1977—I sat there and let this French perm burn through my cerebral cortex rather than tell this man, 'It's hurting.' I told myself, 'Oprah, be a good sport. This man must know what he's doing.' What he did was burn my hair right off!"

Oprah has since gotten a lot of comedy out of the event, but it was traumatizing at the time. She told Mike Wallace when interviewed on *60 Minutes* "It all fell out. Every little strand. I was left with three spriggles in the front. [Wallace laughs] Funny to you! They tried to change me, and then they're stuck with a bald black anchorwoman. I went through a real period of self-discovery, because you have to find other reasons for appreciating yourself. It's certainly not your looks."

Oprah's time in Baltimore was miserable. Due mainly to a failed four-year relationship with a man, she found herself feeling terribly alone and isolated. "I had so much going for me, but I still thought I was nothing without a man . . . I thought I was nothing without him. The more he rejected me, the more I wanted him. I felt depleted, powerless. Once I stayed in bed for three days, missing work; I just couldn't get up. Sad, ain't it!"

In 1981, Oprah was so terribly depressed that she considered committing suicide, even going so far as to compose a note she addressed to a friend. In the note, she told her friend where to find her important papers and asked her to take care of the plants in her apartment. She looks back on those days and is angry at herself for allowing a man to have such power over her. "It was emotional abuse, which happens to women who stay in relationships that do not allow them to be all that they can be. You're not getting knocked around physically, but in terms of your ability to soar, your wings are clipped." Winfrey has dealt with this topic again and again on her show.

Many years after writing the suicide note, she came across an entry in her diary from the time that said simply, "I'm depressed. I want to die." She found herself mourning for the person she had once been. Years later, on a show tackling the problem of drugs, Winfrey revealed that she had used cocaine for several years due to her boyfriend: "I was not addicted," she said. "It was something I did for a short period with a particular boyfriend. I thought he communicated better with me [when we used cocaine], I thought he was more open and more loving."

The admission turned out to be another opportunity for unscrupulous journalists to exploit Winfrey's past mistakes. She describes her use of drugs as her second most shameful secret, the first being her teenage pregnancy. The fact that she had used drugs in an attempt to gain love from a man helped many people in her audience understand that drug use is often a symptom of other, deeper problems. No doubt many people sought help with drug problems thanks to Winfrey's honesty and her willingness to accept the public criticism she was bound to face following her admission. Winfrey was stunned and insulted when some journalists suggested she had revealed her secret simply to get better ratings. After all, by that time, in 1995, she had reached the peak of her profession and had nothing to gain from her admission.

TAKING ON PHIL DONAHUE

Back in 1984, Phil Donahue was one of the most popular personalities on television. Nearly everyone in the United States who turned on their TV in the morning watched his show. Donahue had changed the way talk shows were done. Previously, a celebrity guest sat on stage and was interviewed by a host. The studio audience applauded when the show began, laughed at the jokes, applauded when the guest said something "meaningful" and again during the closing credits. Other than that, they were invisible.

Phil Donahue was known for taking his talk show into the audience. Winfrey credits him for changing television's attitude toward daytime female viewers.

Donahue began doing shows about regular people with ordinary problems, seemingly "normal" people with strange problems, and everything in between. More important, he discussed issues such as racism and sexism. Donahue's genius was to allow members of the audience to question guests, speak out on issues, or offer advice—polite or rude—to the people on stage. Meanwhile, Donahue scurried up and down the aisles with a cordless microphone, adding his own commentary on the fly. With his thick white hair, liberal ideas, pleasant personality, and willingness to tackle difficult subject matter, Donahue became a dominant force in broadcasting and American life.

During this time, Winfrey was working in Baltimore, and Chicago's ABC affiliate had a job opening to fill. They needed someone to host a show that would air at the same time each day as *Donahue*. ABC's executives assumed their show, *A.M. Chicago*, would get trounced in the ratings no matter who was the host. Oprah Winfrey, who had been a hit in Baltimore, applied for the job. Many people in Chicago's local TV industry believed the city was not ready for a black talk-show host, particularly one who was female and overweight. Ignoring such worries, Winfrey flew to town for an interview. She was not optimistic about her chances; she was not even sure she wanted the "opportunity" to go up against Donahue. But there was one thing Winfrey knew immediately: she loved Chicago. "I set foot in this city and just walking down the street, it was like roots, like the motherland. I knew I belonged here."

And she hit it off with her potential boss. "So when I was interviewed . . . I told my boss, 'You know I'm black, and that's not going to change.' He said, 'Yup, I'm lookin' at ya.' I said, 'Yeah, well, and I have this weight problem, too.' And he says, 'Yeah, well, and so do I. So I'm not going to hold that against you. . . .'"

In January 1984, Winfrey became the host of *A.M. Chicago*. She remembers that nearly everyone warned her against taking the job. "Chicago is a racist city!" they argued. Or, "There's no way you can compete with Donahue!" Only her best friend, Gayle King Bumpus, told her she could be a success in Chicago. "Gayle said, 'Leave Baltimore! I *know* you can beat Donahue!'" Bumpus was so enthusiastic that Winfrey almost believed her.

And Bumpus was right. Actually, Winfrey believes the fact she was black might actually have helped her in the Chicago ratings battle. Asked by a local reporter how she had overcome so much perceived racism in Chicago, she said, "There aren't a lot of black people in the Chicago media, and I'm the only one doing what I'm doing. When I came on the air here, it was like you could

Winfrey taking a moment in her office while host of A.M. Chicago

hear TVs clicking on all over the city." Fellow television personality Maury Povich thinks otherwise. Povich believes that Winfrey connected with viewers because she revealed herself: "The closest thing that Phil Donahue ever talked about was the fact he was a wayward Catholic. Oprah opened up a lot of new windows because [women] could empathize with her." Ultimately, Winfrey was a powerful, intelligent woman speaking to other women. Women who worked at home and turned on the TV during the day did not see enough women talking about issues they cared about.

Whatever the reasons, Winfrey was an immediate success in Chicago. But she still felt insecure about her new job. And when Winfrey was under stress, she made herself relax and feel better with food—lots of it.

Already heavy, she quickly gained another 20 pounds (9 kg) in her new job! "I thought I was handling the stress just fine. The show was going well. I was doing great. Everyone told me how easy I made it all look. But underneath I was terrified. So at night I'd sit up all alone in my room at the Knickerbocker Hotel and order French onion soup by the gallon. 'Oh, and could you fry up a cheese sandwich to go with that?' That's how I was handling things."

Despite Winfrey's personal battle with food, nerves, and men, she was doing a terrific job on camera and *A.M. Chicago* was a hit. Winfrey was a natural at the talk-show format. She believes her "instant" success was due to her willingness to look stupid or emotionally needy. She let audience members help her, just as much as she helped them. "Vulnerability is the key: people appreciate when you can be honest. It lets them feel more comfortable about being themselves."

She also acknowledged a huge debt to Phil Donahue for changing television's attitude toward the audience of women who watch television during the day. "Without Donahue, my show wouldn't be possible," she said. "He showed that women have an interest in things that affect their lives and not just how to stuff a cabbage. Because of that I have nothing to prove,

"Without Donahue, my show wouldn't be possible. . . ."

only to do good shows . . . I say, he's the king and I just want a little piece of the kingdom."

During her first few shows, producers supplied Winfrey with questions written on cards. Guests had already supplied their answers to these questions. The idea was that such predictability would allow the show to go smoothly. But Winfrey found she was unable to work with anything scripted: "It just doesn't work for me. It throws me totally off balance. How can I ask a question if I already know the answer? I look like I'm faking it." *A.M. Chicago*'s producers grew to trust Winfrey's abilities. They knew Winfrey was a gifted performer and gave her free reign to choose topics and guests for the show.

During those early years, she interviewed two of her idols: Barbara Walters and Maya Angelou. Tongue-tied and star struck, she found those interviews to be among the most difficult of her career.

In 1985, Winfrey interviewed a group of white-robed women who were members of the Ku Klux Klan, a group dedicated to hatred of blacks, Jews, and other minorities. Winfrey made a real effort to understand what made these women so full of hatred. Millions of viewers were impressed with her calmness, intelligence, and unwillingness to allow these racist women to make her lash out in anger. Others felt Winfrey was not tough enough with these awful people. They felt Winfrey should have "put them in their place." Typical of Winfrey's playfulness, good humor, and desire to change people for the better was a moment near the end of the show when she invited her mean-spirited guests out to lunch. When they declined she added with a smile, "Not even if I pay?"

In 1987, she would display similar grace on a televised visit to all-white Forsyth County, Georgia. "Why come [here]?" she told her viewers. "To explore people's feelings. To ask, 'Why?'" Racism exists, she reasons, so why not bring it to light and try to convince people it is wrong?

CHAPTER FIVE

PROFESSIONAL SUCCESS

In September 1985, *A.M. Chicago* was renamed *The Oprah Winfrey Show.* Winfrey had proven something about changing attitudes toward race in the United States. All those who said white people would not tune in to watch a show hosted by a black woman were shown to be wrong.

"Chicago is one of the most racially volatile cities anywhere. Our success there shows that race and sex can be transcended," she said. That transcendence came because of Winfrey's deep understanding of, and respect for, the hopes and dreams of average people. If nothing else, Winfrey's various personal revelations and struggles, along with her deep intelligence and empathy, have given white people who do not personally know many black people a glimpse of a human truth: whatever race they happen to be, people share the same basic human desires to be happy, safe, and loved.

A new contract meant a huge raise for Winfrey and she immediately began giving some of it away. One of her many projects was the formation of a Big Sister group with members of her staff and two dozen teenage girls from a Chicago public housing project. Looking at these girls, Winfrey saw her former self as she was in Milwaukee. She did not mince words with them. "I shoot a very straight shot: 'Get pregnant and I'll break your face! Don't tell me you want to do great things in your life and still not be able to tell a boy no. You want something to love and to hug? Tell me and I'll get you a puppy!'" Winfrey felt that building self-esteem was the key to saving these girls from the pitfalls of sex, drugs, and crime. Generous with her time and money, Winfrey regularly took the girls to the library and then to the movies or on a shopping spree. Still, she often despaired over their fate. "We have twenty-four in our group. Maybe we'll save two."

THE COLOR PURPLE

As a girl, *I Know Why the Caged Bird Sings* and *Jubilee* had been books Winfrey read again and again. Later in life, *The Color Purple* by Alice

Alice Walker, author of The Color Purple

Walker became another such favorite. Written in the form of letters, the story details the lives of a poor black rural family, more specifically the hardships of the family's women. Winfrey began giving the book to friends and family. "If you got married, you got a copy. If you had a baby, you got a copy. If you divorced, you got a copy. I thought it was one of the best books I had ever read."

When she heard the rights to the book had been purchased by filmmaker Steven Spielberg (*E.T., Jurassic Park, Schindler's List,* and many others) she prayed she would get a chance to audition for a part in the film. "I prayed at night. 'Dear God, find me a way to get into this movie!' I would have done anything, 'best boy,' or 'water girl.'" In fact, she sat down and wrote a letter to author Alice Walker, who was connected to the project, begging her for a chance at a part. But it was pure luck that brought her to the big screen.

Composer, musician, and producer Quincy Jones had just agreed to work with Spielberg on the film when he happened to be passing through Chicago. One morning while flipping television channels in his hotel room, he came across *A.M. Chicago.* "The moment I saw Oprah Winfrey, I knew she would play Sofia," he said.

Soon, Winfrey's secretary handed her a message asking her to go to Hollywood for a screen test. Winfrey was packed and on the next plane to Cal-

Quincy Jones knew Winfrey would be perfect for the role of Sofia in The Color Purple.

ifornia. "The greatest moment of my life was when Steven told me . . . [I] had the part. . . . Maybe the day I was born was greater, but I can't remember that experience." She played the part of Sofia, a woman damaged by abuse who nevertheless maintains her strength and dignity. Near the end of the film, in a speech hauntingly like her own life, she says, "All my life I had to fight. I had to fight my daddy, I had to fight my uncles, I had to fight my brothers. A child ain't safe in a family of mens."

For Winfrey, the character of Sofia represented a long line of African-American women who had struggled for justice throughout U.S. history: "I had Fannie Lou Hamer [a rural Mississippi civil rights fighter of the 1960s] in the back of my head. I thought of her being in and out of jail, so brutalized. I'm aware of my legacy, which is why I was so honored to play Sofia. She was part of all those women I'd been carrying around inside me for years. In high school oratory contests, while everybody else did a speech from *Inherit the Wind*, I'd be doing something from Margaret Walker's *Jubilee*, about a slave woman after the Civil War, or Sojourner Truth's 'Ain't I a Woman?' speech." Winfrey felt a responsibility to live up to the book and to everything she connected with the character of Sofia. "For the first time in my life, I thought, 'What if I do my best and it's just not good enough?'"

Winfrey in The Color Purple

Playing a character in a film was a huge switch for Winfrey, whose show is based on being as much herself as possible. She benefited from working with experienced actors and was happy to take direction from Spielberg. She became more and more comfortable with her role. Gradually, she got over being awestruck by Spielberg and the other actors. "It was a spiritual involvement. I learned to love people doing that film."

Even before the film was released, it was controversial. Many African-Americans were upset

Steven Spielberg offering direction to
Whoopi Goldberg while shooting The Color Purple

that Spielberg, a white man, was directing it. How could he truly understand the African-American slave's experience? What right did he have to tell this story? Other people felt that Alice Walker's novel portrayed all black men as bad. They worried that the last thing African-American men needed was more bad publicity. Already they were often unfairly stereotyped as criminals, or "gangbangers," or just lazy.

Winfrey rejected such arguments. The novel's story, she believed, was not only a "black" story. "It's about endurance, survival, faith, and ultimate triumph." And she resented the argument that the story put black men in a bad light. She pointed out that the narrative was about women, not men. Violence against women and sexual abuse of children was Walker's subject matter. "I tell people that the movie is not for or against men. It's egotistical and macho for men to even think it's about them. *The Color Purple* is a novel about women."

Audiences flocked to and were moved by the movie. It was nominated for eleven Academy Awards, including Winfrey's nomination for Best Supporting Actress. Whoopi Goldberg and Margaret Avery also received nominations. The film did not win a single Oscar, which angered Winfrey. But she was almost glad she herself did not win for Best Supporting Actress. Through a series of mistakes, her gown had been sewn wrong and was much too tight. She actually had to put in on while lying down and had great difficulty in standing up or walking. In fact, aside from getting to sit next to her favorite actor, Jack Nicholson, at the luncheon, she had little fun at the Oscars.

THE OPRAH WINFREY SHOW GOES COAST TO COAST

On September 8, 1986, five years to the day after she wrote her suicide note in Baltimore, Oprah Winfrey became the first black woman ever to host a nationally syndicated television program. Just six months later, *The Oprah Winfrey Show* became the number-one-rated daytime talk show, surpassing *Donahue.*

In the past, Winfrey might have been pleased simply to have come that far. But she began to realize that she now had some real power to change things in television. She wanted to make television more responsive to what was really going on in people's lives. She wanted to change the way African-Americans and women were portrayed. Also she hoped to do something to curb the mind-numbing barrage of violence shown hour after hour to America's young people. Such "fake" violence, many believe, desensitizes people to real violence and promotes the idea of settling conflicts with force instead of discussion and compromise.

Winfrey at Harpo Studios

Winfrey used her new wealth to found Harpo Entertainment Group, whose divisions include Harpo Productions, Harpo Studios, and Harpo Films. (Harpo is Oprah spelled backward.) She stated Harpo's mission as follows: "In a society so media controlled, doing good films is one of the best ways to raise consciousness." Winfrey purchased a block-long building in a run-down section of Chicago and spent $20 million to make it a state-of-the-art facility with three sound stages and offices for all of her staff.

Before Winfrey, only comedienne Lucille Ball and silent film star Mary Pickford were female studio owners. Winfrey became the first African-American woman to be one. It is easy to discount the importance of this fact, but television and films help shape the way we think about the world. Because much of our daily information and entertainment come from television, TV executives wield tremendous power. Whoever is in control of what gets shown on TV helps to determine not only our opinions about various issues, but which issues will even be seen at all.

In the case of African-Americans, television has arguably done a poor job "seeing" the reality of their diverse lives. For the most part, they have been invisible. Winfrey sums up the media's portrayal of African-Americans like this: "Most people out there have no contact with black people ever. Their only images are the ones portrayed on television. . . . There's a whole reality outside of what most people know, where the black community functions on its own, where people own businesses, where people care about prosperity and their children and pay their taxes. The point of having your own company is that you can show that." Too often, the only African-Americans upon which television focuses are sports and singing stars and criminals.

Because of the incredible influence of television, Oprah Winfrey and Bill Cosby must be ranked with Reverend Jesse Jackson and General Colin Powell as among the most influential black leaders of the 1980s and 1990s. All are viewed by a majority of black *and* white people as positive role models.

HARPO ENTERTAINMENT GROUP

The first thing Harpo did in 1988 was buy *The Oprah Winfrey Show* from ABC television for $20 million. This gave Oprah Winfrey complete control of the content and direction of the show. Though she planned always to make *The Oprah Winfrey Show* her continued priority, she was also excited about new projects. She decided that the first film Harpo Films made would be based on Gloria Naylor's novel *The Women of Brewster Place*. Like *The Color Purple*, the book had touched Winfrey deeply with its portrayal of strong black women struggling to survive.

Although Harpo Films gave Winfrey the power to create any television programming she thought was important, she still had to convince one of the networks to buy and broadcast it. ABC, NBC, and CBS are controlled in large part by men who—while they might be very sympathetic to the causes of minorities—must sell commercial airtime to corporations. These corporations, such as McDonald's, Microsoft, or Wal-Mart, must be con-

Starring in The Women of Brewster Place

vinced that a lot of viewers will tune in to a given program before they will pay millions of dollars for commercial time. So, in general, TV executives will only buy and show programs likely to draw huge audiences. The wrong choice can be a costly disaster for the network. All these nervous executives initially turned *Brewster Place* down. "They said it was too womanish. I said, 'Look, I know you are very wise and perceptive men and the only reason you have turned down this project is because you haven't read the book. You could not read it and turn it down. I'll be calling on you Tuesday to see who's read it.' Only one wise, perceptive executive had read the book by the deadline, but he was sold."

When Oprah saw the final cut of the project, she was overjoyed. "I am very, very proud of it," she said. She also loved working with her fellow actresses. The cast of 150 included Cicely Tyson and Robin Givens. "It was an incredible experience. I haven't done a lot of acting and I really enjoyed it. I love women, and working with these women was wonderful, because they are all so wonderful." The effort was a hit, the highest-rated miniseries of the 1988–1989 television season. Winfrey's only regret about the miniseries was her own physical appearance. "I can't believe I was that big!" she said.

Winfrey's strong performance was all the more impressive because it was only the fourth time she had acted. She found acting a challenge: "I guess I'm a natural, but I'm very short on technique. I actually live the moment, almost like channeling the character. . . ." She did a lot of writing about her character, imagining an entire life's history for Mattie, so that when the time came to portray Mattie, Winfrey drew on all sorts of imagined past experiences. Though this method of preparation produced an excellent performance, Winfrey found it to be a difficult way to go about the job of acting. "By the end of the day, when it's time for the close-up, I'm just emotionally whipped. Unless I can actually feel the pain I think I didn't do it right. But you can't feel it for twelve takes."

When Winfrey tried to make Brewster Place the setting for a regular series, the show flopped and was canceled after just ten airings. She had rushed ahead with the project before it was ready. She later recognized her mistakes: "[It] wasn't the time and I wasn't willing to listen to the instinct that said, 'Wait.' I should have waited. I was anxious."

TESTIFYING BEFORE CONGRESS

Winfrey's next performance was perhaps her most remarkable to date. On November 12, 1991, Winfrey stood before members of the U.S. Senate speaking in support of a bill to protect children from sex offenders.

It was not her own past that brought her to Washington, D.C., but a terrible story she saw on the television news one night. A four-year-old Chicago girl had been kidnapped, raped, murdered, and then dumped into Lake Michigan. Incredibly, the man who committed this evil crime had already been convicted and sent to prison for raping two other children before his latest victim. "I didn't know the child," Winfrey said later. "Never heard her laughter. But I vowed that night to do something."

> **"I didn't know the child. Never heard her laughter. But I vowed that night to do something."**

Winfrey and former Illinois Governor James Thompson teamed up to write a bill called the National Child Protection Act. The proposed law called for creation of an FBI databank of all convicted sex offenders. Such a resource would allow police to better protect the nation's children from predators.

Winfrey testified strongly on behalf of children vulnerable to such attacks by strangers, neighbors, even relatives. She told the Senate Judiciary Committee: "I wept for Angela [the murdered girl] and I wept for us, a society that apparently cares so little about its children that we would allow a man with two previous convictions [for the] kidnapping and rape of children to go free

*Winfrey and former Illinois Governor
James Thomspon looking on as President Bill
Clinton signs the National Child Protection
Act in December 1993*

after serving only seven years of a fifteen-year sentence."

Thompson was impressed with Winfrey's drive to succeed: "When millions of people look to you, it empowers you to do more than you ordinarily might. This is a woman with extraordinary commitment." The bill easily passed in the Congress. On December 20, 1993, Winfrey stood beside President Bill Clinton as he signed the bill into law.

Winfrey continues to raise public awareness concerning the abuse of children. "You lose your childhood when you've been abused. My heart goes out to those children who are abused at home and have no one to turn to." When documentary filmmaker Arnold Schapiro asked Winfrey to participate in the making of a documentary about child abuse in the United States, Winfrey agreed immediately. All three networks agreed to air the important and moving program in part because it was hosted by Winfrey. The networks, she said, "understand that this is important enough to overlook ratings, overlook revenues, and just get the message out and try and help as many people as we can."

THE RISE OF HARPO ENTERTAINMENT GROUP

Harpo's next production after *The Women of Brewster Place* was a true-life drama called *There Are*

No Children Here. Based on Alex Kotlowitz's book of the same name, the film was shot on location at Chicago's Henry Horner Homes. The Henry Horner Homes is a low-income housing project on Chicago's crime-ridden west side. Winfrey played a good mother struggling to hold her family together and keep her children safe in the face of gang violence, crime, drugs, and apathy.

Winfrey donated her entire $500,000 salary to a scholarship fund set up to help Henry Horner's children go to college. After spending a summer in Henry Horner, Winfrey found herself becoming attached to the families she met. She came to realize that even she had a stereotyped image of those who live in public housing, especially the young people. "I used to see these kids from the projects walking down the street and think, 'Oh, my god, is something going to happen?' Now I look to see if it's one of the kids I know. That's the difference."

Near the end of the filming, the pastor of a local church thanked Winfrey and her staff for providing a bit of hope for residents. "I just wanted to weep when he said that, because I realized, looking into the faces of those children, that's exactly what we had done."

Despite working in the glamorous world of show business, Winfrey refuses to ignore the suffering that goes on around her. Again and again, she demonstrates an ability to feel pain when oth-

Starring in There Are No Children Here, *with Mark Lane (right) and Norman Golden II (left)*

ers are feeling pain, and joy when they are happy. Remarking on her summer in Henry Horner she said, "You find people in the projects who have as much desire for fulfillment and enrichment—to be somebody—as [people] anywhere else in the world. The lesson is that we really are all the same and it doesn't matter how you're packaged. The heart is always the same." True, Winfrey left the bleak high-rises of Henry Horner in her limousine each night and slept in an $850,000 apartment on Michigan Avenue. But this is not an irony that she ignores. Winfrey never fails to see herself as a person connected to a community outside the world of television and movies. She also rarely fails to use the power of television constructively, to shed light on real problems faced by real people—people who do not live in the world of situation comedy where problems are solved in the last five minutes with a quick hug and a kind word. Winfrey focuses on the sort of problems that have "been around forever." Seen by many as unsolvable, these nagging miseries are often ignored.

CHAPTER SIX

HITTING THE BIG TIME

In 1991, Winfrey earned $40 million and had $250 million in assets. By 1992, *Forbes* magazine reported that Winfrey and Bill Cosby were the two wealthiest entertainers in the world. Winfrey made $88 million in the two years of 1990 and 1991. She used some of her cash to acquire movie rights to various books she loved. Today, Harpo Entertainment Group owns the rights to Zora Neal Hurstons's *Their Eyes Were Watching God* and Mark Mathabane's *Kaffir Boy*, his memoir of his South African boyhood under apartheid.

Winfrey's commitment to quality caused her to cancel publication of her autobiography in 1994. She felt that although the book was well written and captured the details of her life, it was not the sort of book that would empower people. It did not seem to offer any lessons on how to live. She felt it was too early for her book. "I am in the heart of a learning curve. I feel there are important discoveries yet to be made," she explained. Knowing that Knopf (her publisher) and many other people would be disappointed with her decision made it all the more difficult. She continues to work on the manuscript.

STEDMAN GRAHAM

"He's kind and he's supportive, and he's six feet six inches [198 cm]!" Winfrey began a relationship with Stedman Graham, Jr., in 1986, and the question posed by nosy reporters ever since has been whether or when they will be married. From the beginning, Winfrey's incredible celebrity made the relationship difficult. Reporters speculated that Graham, tall and handsome, simply wanted to use Winfrey to begin an acting career. "Nothing could be further from the truth," Winfrey said. "He hates the limelight." Soon, rumors surfaced that Graham was a homosexual. Winfrey was convinced this rumor began simply because she was overweight. Many people believed that a handsome, straight man could never be attracted to an overweight woman. "He just plain sees me, not the size," she explained.

One painful memory Winfrey recalls in her 1997 videotape *Make the Connection* involves such cruel thinking. She remembers walking into

Winfrey with longtime boyfriend, Stedman Graham

a gala fund-raiser with Graham and overhearing a woman say to her friend, "She may have all that money and that handsome man, but she's also got a fat butt!"

Graham and Winfrey announced in 1992 that they planned to be married someday and have a family. To date, the relationship remains constantly studied by tabloid journalists looking for a juicy story. Winfrey claims that stories about breakups and reunifications are "simply not true." For several years Winfrey's history of troubles with men made her hesitant to get married. "Neither of us is ready. It really bothers me that people think it's either he doesn't want me or I don't want him." She often describes Stedman Graham as being the opposite of all the men who have mistreated her during her life.

Winfrey also worries about motherhood. "Sometimes I think, yes, I do want to have that experience. And other times I must admit having a child is not a deep yearning at this time. Maybe I'm afraid. Raising a child is such serious business."

Winfrey's long courtship with Stedman, as she refers to him on her shows, has been yet another learning experience she has shared with the public. Today she, Graham, and Solomon (a cocker spaniel) live together in a magnificent penthouse condominium overlooking Lake Michigan. The three also share vacations at Winfrey's

162-acre (65.5-hectare) farm in Indiana or her ranch near Telluride, Colorado.

WINFREY'S STRUGGLE WITH WEIGHT

Where Winfrey is concerned, far more attention has been paid to the size of her rear end than to the color of her skin. Perhaps only movie star Elizabeth Taylor has been the subject of more size-related talk than Oprah Winfrey.

In her early days as a talk-show host, she grew larger because she used eating to relieve stress. During the mid-1980's, Winfrey's weight fluctuated wildly. At one point in 1988, she entered the studio in a skintight pair of jeans pulling behind her a wagon loaded with 67 pounds (30 kg) of lard to represent the weight she had lost. But that remarkable rapid weight loss was accomplished through a liquid diet, and she soon gained it all back—and then some. Oprah's on-air struggle with obesity matched the struggles of millions of viewers. "It is an obsession. It's all an overweight woman talks about. It just happens that I'm in the public eye, so people think I talk about it more."

Winfrey's problems with food were more emotional than physical. She began to realize that if she dealt with her emotional pain, she would not need food as a comfort. "Obviously I have used

Oprah Winfrey has had to battle a weight problem for much of her life.

food in the past to suppress my feelings rather than confront them. Even now it's hard not to. Having been a food addict, I can identify with the woman who is an alcoholic. I really, really under-

Winfrey and a wagon loaded with lard, which was meant to represent the weight she had lost in 1988

stand people's pain." She added later that her "greatest failure was believing that the weight issue was just about weight. Dieting is not about weight. It's about everything else that's not going right in your life."

Besides understanding the nature of her eating problem, Winfrey began to exercise regularly. This fitness program led to her running the Marine Corps Marathon in 1994. "I never felt anything like the sense of accomplishment I had when I finished the marathon. . . . But it's not really the race that mattered. It was the training, the discipline that it took to keep going for so many weeks beforehand." Winfrey not only finished the grueling 26-mile (42-km) course, her time was quite impressive as well.

Winfrey also received help from a chef named Rosie Daley. On one of her frequent trips to a health spa where she went in hopes of quickly losing weight, Winfrey sat down to dinner and had a revelation. The meal she ate was delicious, spicy, and satisfying, yet contained only 300 calories. She immediately went to the kitchen to meet Rosie Daley, the woman who had prepared the meal. During the next few days, as she ate one

"Dieting is not about weight. It is about everything else that's not going right in your life."

fabulous meal after another, Winfrey convinced Daley to move to Chicago and become her personal cook.

In 1994, Winfrey and Daley released a cookbook called *In the Kitchen with Rosie: Oprah's Favorite Recipes*. An instant best-seller, the book encourages what Winfrey calls "clean eating." This means eating meals low in fat and calories that taste good and make you feel good after you eat them. "Real cooking is an art form, a gift to be shared," wrote Winfrey in the book's foreword. To date, 5 million copies of the cookbook have been sold.

A NEW DIRECTION

By the time Oprah Winfrey was forty years old in 1995, she was on her way to becoming the first African-American *billionaire* in U.S. history. As host of the nation's most popular TV talk show for eight consecutive years, she and her staff had won more Emmy Awards than they had shelves to put them on. But she was disturbed by what she saw happening to her show and her many imitators. Struggling to grab viewers away from one another, Winfrey, Jerry Springer, Sally Jessy Raphaël, and almost countless others catered to the lowest common denominator. It seemed every show featured cheap and sleazy topics designed to lure an audience at any cost. Winfrey considered quitting

*Taking home a daytime Emmy Award for
outstanding talk show host, May 1994*

the talk-show game altogether. Instead, she
pledged to focus her energies and airtime on
meaningful and uplifting topics. If the show lost
ratings in the process, she decided, she would
quit. But, believing her core audience was intelligent and thoughtful, she would no longer lower

herself to compete for ratings. She began to feature more psychologists, authors, and people who were positive role models.

Winfrey devoted most of the 1996 season to a series called "Oprah's Child Alert." The series tackled issues affecting the nation's young people, particularly low-income children. Gun violence, poverty, and abuse were openly discussed by experts and average citizens. Sometimes possible solutions were examined, but often guests simply talked about what was really happening in the schoolyards, streets, and homes around them. Again and again, Winfrey called upon everyone, and particularly women, to empower themselves to escape bad situations, to save their children, to take control of their lives and make a difference.

At the end of the 1995–1996 television season, Winfrey received the George Foster Peabody Individual Achievement Award, the most prestigious honor in broadcasting. *Time* magazine recognized her as one of "America's 25 Most Influential People of 1996."

MAKE THE CONNECTION

In 1997, Winfrey released a special videotape called *Make the Connection* (a book of the same title was published the year before). Created with Bob Greene, her personal trainer, the tape asks

Promoting her 1996 book, Make the Connection

viewers to understand that weight problems are usually connected to many other issues in their lives, especially low self-esteem, the inability to love oneself. Food can become a kind of medicine used to ease emotional pain. Winfrey reveals the true depth of the pain she suffered as an obese person. She tearfully remembers not wanting to win an Emmy Award simply so she would not have to get up out of her chair and be looked at by millions of people. She describes her desperate worries over how she would make the long walk from her seat to the podium without embarrassing herself. Another low point came when she went to a heavyweight championship boxing match and learned that she and champion Mike Tyson both tipped the scales at 218 pounds (99 kg)!

Ultimately, *Make the Connection* is about far more than eating low-fat food and exercising regularly. It suggests a way to change your life, to become the person you dream of being. By the end of the tape, we understand just what it meant to Winfrey to finish that marathon. It was as if she had finally outrun the nightmares of her childhood for good. Winfrey donated her share of profits from the popular tape to charity.

A MEATY ISSUE

In 1996, the world learned of a frightening disease affecting cattle in England. It was discovered that proteins in the bones and meat of sick animals could be passed on to humans. So-called "mad cow disease" slowly destroys the brain of the victim and ultimately causes death. Winfrey and her producers decided to examine the topic. During the show, Winfrey and the audience learned from one expert that the practice of feeding ground-up animal parts to cattle could theoretically spread the disease to humans in the United States.

Horrified by this possibility, Winfrey exclaimed: "It has just stopped me from eating another burger!" The audience applauded wildly.

The reaction of U.S. cattle producers was less favorable. They were even more unhappy when the price of beef in the United States dropped to a ten-year low. They claimed part of this panic was due to Winfrey's influence over housewives who still do most of the grocery shopping in the United States. They pointed to the incredible success of Oprah's Book Club as an example of her clout. Each month or so, Winfrey selects a book she has enjoyed or felt was important. Any title chosen for the club becomes an instant best-seller.

Texas cattlemen decided to sue Winfrey for damages caused by what they said was "unfair and biased coverage of the issue." Mad cow disease had never been detected in the United States. In 1998, Winfrey admitted in court that the show could have been better researched but argued that she never intentionally attacked the

OPRAH'S BOOK CLUB

A selected list of some of Oprah's selections and her announcement dates:

I Know This Much Is True by Wally Lamb. June 18, 1998

Black and Blue by Anna Quindlen. April 9, 1998

Here on Earth by Alice Hoffman. March 6, 1998

Paradise by Toni Morrison. January 16, 1998

The Best Way to Play by Bill Cosby. December 8, 1997

Ellen Foster by Kaye Gibbons. October 27, 1997

The Heart of a Woman by Maya Angelou. May 9, 1997

The Rapture of Canaan by Sheri Reynolds. April 8, 1997

The Book of Ruth by Jane Hamilton. November 19, 1996

The Deep End of the Ocean by Jacquelyn Mitchard. September 17, 1996

cattle industry. Lawyers for the Texas cattlemen had to prove that she had meant to harm sales of beef.

Not only did Winfrey win the case, but a week of shows done in Texas endeared her to most people in the state. "I am grateful for the kindness of

*Winfrey celebrating her victory over the Texas
cattlemen in a 1998 court case*

strangers," she said. "I'll miss Amarillo." Winfrey's
schedule in Texas included forty-one long days in
court and long nights taping the show. "I wouldn't
have chosen this experience," she said after hear-
ing the verdict. "I believe that in life, experiences

take you to a place you would not name, and I would not have named Amarillo."

It is a perfect example of Oprah Winfrey's gift that she can enter a place where she is despised, meet her "enemies" face to face, and create a new group of friends.

BELOVED

> *124 was spiteful. Full of baby's venom. The women in the house knew it and so did the children.*

So begins Toni Morrison's 1987 novel *Beloved*. Morrison, one of the world's greatest living writers, won the Nobel Prize for literature in 1997, and she is one of Winfrey's heroes. After Winfrey read the book, she became absolutely convinced that she had to play its main character. Sethe is a runaway slave whose house is haunted by the ghost of her murdered baby daughter. "I finished reading the book and never doubted . . . I just felt it."

Winfrey had ten years to prepare for the role. *Beloved* was not an easy story to make into a film. Morrison's style of writing is very complex. It took finding just the right director and cast to make the story come alive and remain true to the book's messages. Jonathan Demme (*Silence of the Lambs*

Danny Glover with Winfrey in the 1998 film Beloved

and *Philadelphia*) became the director. Danny Glover jumped at the chance to play Paul D, another former slave who finds Sethe living in a house haunted by the past and tries to save her. A group of excellent actors filled the rest of the roles.

At last the first scene was filmed. The movie opens as Sethe runs through a field of yellow chamomile flowers. Winfrey recalled that even as she ran through the field, she could not believe that filming had actually begun. Nothing seemed real to her. She wrote in *Journey to Beloved*, a day-by-day journal of her involvement with the film: "I am a descendant of slaves. I came from nothing. Now I have the freedom, power, and will to speak for millions every day."

> **"I am a descendant of slaves. I came from nothing. Now I have the freedom, power, and will to speak for millions every day."**

The film version of *Beloved*, like the book, does not always directly show the horrible effects of slavery. Instead, the movie uses dream images to convey a sense of sadness, loss, and painful memories. In one scene, Sethe's mother-in-law preaches in a forest about the sad fact of slavery and the lesson former slaves were forced to learn:

Here in this here place, we flesh, flesh that weeps, laughs. Flesh that dances on bare feet in grass. Love it. Love it hard. Yonder they do not love your flesh. They despise it. They don't love your eyes, they just as soon pick 'em out. No more do they love the skin on your back. Yonder they flay it. And O my people they do not love your hands. Those they only use, tie, bind, chop off, and leave empty. Love your hands! Love them. Raise them up and kiss them. Touch others with them, pat them together, stroke them on your face 'cause they don't love that either. You got to love it, you!

Throughout the planning stages of *Beloved*, Winfrey insisted the movie be true to the spirit of Toni Morrison's book. As the film's producer, she fought off many attempts to make the movie simpler, more upbeat, easier to understand. Winfrey insisted the movie capture all of the complexities and pain of the book. A film critic for *The New York Times* pointed out that Winfrey deserved praise for having seen to it that Hollywood did not weaken *Beloved*'s powerful story: "Oprah Winfrey and Jonathan Demme have made *Beloved* a movie that will appeal to lovers of Morrison's allusive, poetic novel."

*Oprah Winfrey is known for her generosity
and outgoing personality.*

WINFREY'S GENEROSITY

Oprah Winfrey gives away a lot of money. She has established hundreds of scholarship funds at colleges and universities throughout the United States. Each year, she helps 100 African-American men attend Morehouse College in Atlanta, Georgia. She endows ten annual scholarships in her father's name at Tennessee State University.

Winfrey is also well known for lavishing gifts on friends and employees. She wrote buddy Gayle King Bumpus, who currently has her own talk show, a check for $1.25 million one year for Christmas. In 1987, she took three of the show's producers and her publicist on a wild shopping spree at Bergdorf's department store. The four women were allowed to buy all they could carry during a one-hour shopping frenzy. No wonder she inspires loyalty. "I would take a bullet for her," remarked producer Mary Kay Clinton.

WINFREY'S SPIRITUALITY

"I am guided by a higher calling," Winfrey has explained. "It's not so much a voice as a feeling. If it doesn't feel right to me, I don't do it." Winfrey feels a deep and daily connection to God. "I am convinced that the difference between how I handle my life and how [some] other people handle theirs is that I don't just pray, I truly heed the response I am given. My friend Maya Angelou told me a while back that she thought one of my greatest assets is my ability to be obedient to the voice of God within me and I think she's right."

CHRONOLOGY

1954	Is born on January 29 in Kosciusko, Mississippi
1960	Is sent to Wilwaukee, Wisconsin, to live with her mother and half-sister
1968	Is sent by her mother to Nashville, Tennessee, to live with her father and step-mother
1971	Becomes the first African-American to win Miss Fire Prevention beauty pageant in Nashville; is hired to read the news for station WVOL
1972	Wins the Miss Black Nashville pageant; graduates from East High School; wins Miss Black Tennessee pageant; enters Tennessee State University
1973	Is hired as weekend news co-anchor at WTVF-TV in Nashville

1976	Is hired as evening news co-anchor at WJZ-TV in Baltimore
1977	Is named host of WJZ-TV's *People Are Talking*
1983	Is hired to host *A.M. Chicago* at WLS-TV
1985	*A.M. Chicago* is renamed *The Oprah Winfrey Show*; stars in Steven Spielberg's *The Color Purple*
1986	Is nominated for Academy Award for Best Supporting Actress for *The Color Purple*; *The Oprah Winfrey Show* is syndicated nationally; forms Harpo Entertainment Group
1987	Earns degree from Tennessee State University; endows ten TSU scholarships in her father's name; *The Oprah Winfrey Show* wins three daytime Emmy Awards; is named Broadcaster of the year by the International Radio and Television Society, the youngest person ever so honored
1988	Produces and stars in TV miniseries *The Women of Brewster Place*
1991	Testifies before the U.S. Senate Judiciary Committee to propose bill providing for national screening system to protect children from sexual predators

1992	Announces engagement to Stedman Graham
1993	Wins Horatio Alger Award for overcoming adversity to become a leader in society; *The Oprah Winfrey Show* wins the Emmy Award for best talk show
1996	Is awarded the George Foster Peabody Award for Individual Achievement, the highest honor in broadcasting; establishes Oprah's Book Club
1997	Stands trial and is cleared of liable charges brought by Texas beef producers; establishes Oprah's Angel Network, aimed at increasing charitable donations by the show's viewers
1998	Produces and stars in the film version of *Beloved*; is named show business's most powerful person by *Entertainment Weekly* magazine

Oprah Winfrey has been much written about, and the basic facts of her life are available via many sources. I used Lois Nicholson's *Oprah Winfrey* and several other biographies to compile the basics. I also read any number of the countless magazine articles both long and short covering much of the same material. Winfrey's official website, www.oprah.com, was somewhat useful as were other general celebrity websites. I used CNN's www.cnn.com for current news about Winfrey. Winfrey's own videotape, *Make the Connection,* proved valuable in understanding Winfrey's outlook on life and her long struggle toward physical and spiritual transformation. I found Bill Adler's *The Uncommon Wisdom of Oprah Winfrey: A Portrait in Her Own Words* and Janet Lowe's *Oprah Winfrey Speaks: Insights from the*

World's Most Influential Woman valuable in the gathering of direct quotes concerning any number of topics.

FOR MORE INFORMATION

BOOKS

Buffalo, Audreen. *Meet Oprah Winfrey*. New York: Random House, 1993.

Greene, Bob, and Oprah Winfrey. *Make the Connection: Ten Steps to a Better Body—and a Better Life*. New York: Hyperion, 1996.

Nicholson, Lois P. *Oprah Winfrey: Entertainer*. Black Americans of Achievement series. New York: Chelsea House, 1994.

Otfinoski, Steven. *Oprah Winfrey: TV Star*. Woodbridge, CT: Blackbirch Press, 1992.

Patterson, Lillie, and Cornelia H. Wright. *Oprah Winfrey: Talk Show Host and Actress*. Contemporary Women series. Hillside, NJ: Enslow Publishers, 1990.

Woods, Geraldine. *The Oprah Winfrey Story: Speaking Her Mind*. Minneapolis: Dillon Press, 1991.

VIDEOTAPE

Greene, Bob, and Oprah Winfrey. *Make the Connection: Ten Steps to a Better Body—and a Better Life.* Chicago: Harpo Communications, 1997.

INTERNET SITES

Celebsite: Oprah Winfrey
http://www.celebsite.com/people/oprah winfrey/
Offers a brief biography of Winfrey, along with links to other related sites.

The Oprah Winfrey Show
http://www.oprah.com
This official Oprah Winfrey site features upcoming shows, biographical information, daily thoughts from Winfrey, and book club information. Also includes bulletin boards where viewers can offer one another advice, support, and often prayers.

Rachel's Ode to Oprah
http://oprah.virtual-space.com/
A fan's tribute to Winfrey that offers a bulletin board and chat room. Also provides information on the Angel Network, Oprah's Book Club, and *The Oprah Winfrey Show.*

Random Acts of Kindness with Oprah Winfrey
http://www.intouchmag.com/kindness.html
This site offers a transcript of Winfrey's show on random acts of kindness and provides suggestions for ways everyone can practice such "random acts." Sponsored by *A Magazine for People and Possibilities*.

THE OPRAH WINFREY SHOW

The Oprah Winfrey Show is generally taped at Harpo Studios on Tuesdays, Wednesdays, and Thursdays at 9:00 A.M. and again at noon. Audience members must be at least sixteen years of age. For reservations, call 312-591-9222 during Chicago's business hours.

INDEX

ABOUT THE AUTHOR

Philip Brooks grew up near Chicago and now lives with his wife, Balinda, in Columbus, Ohio. He attended the Iowa Writers Workshop and has published his fiction in a number of literary journals. He has also published several other works of nonfiction for Franklin Watts and Children's Press including *Extraordinary Jewish Americans, The United States Holocaust Memorial and Museum, Games People Play: Japan, Games People Play: The United States*, and numerous biographies of athletes.